Secrets of Successful Virtual Book Tours

Quick Tips for Authors

Roxanne Rhoads

Secrets of Successful Virtual Book Tours

Copyright © 2016 by Roxanne Rhoads

All rights reserved. No part of this book may be reproduced or transmitted in any form or by any means without written permission of the author.

ISBN 978-1523650286

Table of Contents

Introduction 1
Chapter 1: What Is a Virtual Book Tour? 3
Chapter 2: What To Do Before Your Virtual Book Tour 7
Chapter 3: What To Expect From a Virtual Book Tour 19
Chapter 4: Secrets for a Successful Book Tour 25
Chapter 5: An Author's Guide to Writing Great Guest Blogs .39
Chapter 6: Tips for Planning Your Own Virtual Book Tour ...49
Chapter 7: Are Real World Events Things of the Past? 55
About the Author 57
Afterword: Consider Bewitching Book Tours 59

Introduction

The world of publishing is continuously evolving thanks to technology and the Internet. It is now easier than ever to publish a book. But with the growing number of new books being released every day it is also harder than ever to get your book noticed in the crowd.

If your line of thinking includes- "If I publish it, people will buy it," think again.

Indie publishing requires a dedication to self-promotion. Gone are the days an author hermits them self away to write, then hands the book to the publisher who does all the leg work for promotion. Even NYT Bestselling authors and those with contracts through the big publishers still have to do a certain amount of self-promotion.

There are many ways to promote: social media, advertising on popular websites and blogs, print advertising in trade magazines, attending reader oriented conventions and events…but one of the best ways to get your book out there and build name recognition as an author is through a virtual book tour.

In this Quick Tips for Authors Guide, you will learn why a virtual book tour can be an author's most effective marketing tool.

Chapter 1: What Is a Virtual Book Tour?

Virtual book tours are a way to visit multiple places and get the word out about your book without ever leaving your home. They are a powerful way to gain exposure for your book and your author brand.

You will get the chance to interact directly with readers and future book buyers; you can develop ongoing relationships with media professionals, other authors, book bloggers, and reviewers.

Why Tour?

Virtual book tours are one of the best ways to spread the word about your book because it is relatively easy and you can promote your book around the world without ever leaving your home- and one of the big bonuses of a virtual book tour is that your tour content will remain online.

Most sites keep content live and archived forever (as long as the site exists). That way you can post permalinks on your site to the content and it will stay alive in the virtual world to be shared and enjoyed indefinitely.

Imagine- you can reach a worldwide audience at a tiny fraction of the cost of a real world book tour.

Virtual book tours are perfect for both new authors and established authors with a new release or looking for a boost for a backlist book.

Established authors can showcase their new release to the world, reach new readers, and establish a larger network.

New authors get a grand introduction to the online book world and will be showcased in front of many readers eager for new books to read.

The goal of an online tour should not be increasing book sales but reaching out and gaining new followers. After a book tour, you should have more social media followers, your newsletter subscriber list should have grown and hopefully, your book sales will have increased.

A virtual book tour will build your author platform, boost your website and social media hits, raise your website's Alexa rankings and increase your author visibility on Google.

Virtual book tours may go by many names- virtual tour, online book tour, blog tour…basically they are the same though some may have different components.

Which leads us to - what do you do during a book tour?

Secrets of Successful Virtual Book Tours

You'll write guest posts, fill out and interviews, and sometimes participate in live chats, podcasts, and radio interviews at sites around the web. Some tours may include Facebook events, Twitter parties or Twitterviews (an interview via twitter), google hangout interviews or chats, or webinars.

You can either search for sites to feature your book and schedule everything yourself or hire a tour company to coordinate and schedule everything for you.

If you decide to hire a tour company one key to a successful tour is choosing the best company for your book- find a company that has handled many books in your genre and that showcases a good track record of tours. If you only see one or two previous tours done by this company perhaps you should move on to the next book tour company- and new ones pop up every day. Don't get taken in by cheap prices and big promises.

Do your homework before laying down the cash. While no book tour business can guarantee sales or great reviews they should be able to provide you with proven capability, organization and a certain amount of tour stops based on what you paid for. The best advertising is word of mouth. See what tour companies other authors in your genre have used. Ask other authors about their experiences.

Chapter 2: What To Do Before Your Virtual Book Tour

Before you embark on a tour you should have a basic online and social media presence. This means a website, newsletter and social media accounts that the tour can build upon. A tour can help you gain social media followers and build your newsletter subscriber list.

First of all- create a website.

What's the first thing many people do when they hear about something- whether it's a book, business, or new product?

They Google it.

That's why an author should have a website- a good one, a professional one that showcases their author brand. If you write paranormal books your website should have a hint of the paranormal to it. Should it showcase screaming skulls and blood dripping fangs? Probably not. Keep it tasteful and professional while making it clear you are a paranormal author, or romance author, or whatever.

Your website can sell you and your books 24 hours a day, 7 days a week all over the world. Nothing else can reach as wide of an audience 24/7.

An Author Website Should Contain 6 Key Features:

- Author Contact Info- include your professional author email as well as a contact form.

- Author Bio

- Author Bookshelf (if you write in different genres or have a couple different series then you should have separate pages for each genre or series).

- Calendar or schedule of author appearances both in the real world and online (this is where you will post your virtual tour schedule).

- A page of fun/bonus stuff and/or links that relate to your books- this can be book trailers, book soundtracks, character profiles, and free short stories.

- Media page which should contain an author photo, media ready bio, sample author Q and A, and your most recent book cover and blurb. It is advisable to have a downloadable media kit available. Several virtual book tour companies include professional media kit creation in their tour packages.

An author should also have a regularly updated blog and a newsletter.

You can create free blogs through Blogger, WordPress, and Weebly. You can also easily purchase a domain name through a company like GoDaddy.com and point it to your free site.

The best newsletter service I have used is Mailchimp. Aweber is okay, but Mailchimp is great, especially if you use an Android phone and google based products (Chrome, google drive, Gmail, blogger, etc.).

Be sure to utilize Author Central at Amazon, you can add your links and blog feed to your author page.

Which brings me to the next thing an author needs to utilize…social media- Twitter, Facebook, Google +, Tsu, Pinterest, Goodreads, Tumblr- these are some of the most popular social media outlets for connecting with readers and other authors.

According to Pew Internet Project's Research as of January 2014, 74% of online adults use social networking sites. That's a lot of people to connect with.

The idea is to build a solid foundation of reader and author followers. To quote Rachel Thompson of BadRedhead Media, "social media helps you build relationships that will help you to sell books. Social media is social. It's not one way BUY MY BOOK link blasts. If that's all you are doing, stop it now."

The goal is creating a tribe of like-minded people. If you write paranormal romance, urban fantasy or horror connect with those who love related things like paranormal and sci-fi TV shows and movies. If you are a fan of popular shows like The Walking Dead, Supernatural, The Vampire Diaries, The Originals, Teen Wolf, Dr. Who, etc. seek out the fandoms of these shows. Chances are you can find a few fans that will enjoy your work.

But be sincere, do this by posting fun and informative tweets and updates- not just your book promo. Talk about things you love, things you do, reach out to those interested in the same things. Then occasionally toss in- "my newest book just released" or "My book XYZ is currently on sale".

If keeping track of multiple social media accounts is daunting you can link all accounts together through apps at Twitter and Facebook or through outside apps like HootSuite. One post and it goes to all your social media outlets. However different social media sites are good for different things.

Facebook is great for connecting with people everywhere and building pages for your books and series. Facebook is still my favorite and must have social media outlet even if they've made it hard to promote via pages. I recommend having a page people can visit to learn more about your work, keep it updated with links to your website, other social media accounts, teasers, tour dates, etc. Facebook is also great for events. You can create an event and use it as a live chat to connect with readers in real time.

Twitter is great for quick connects and posting links, but some find it hard to create engaging tweets of 140 characters or less. But once you get the hang of it, it can be quite addicting. Check out #marketingsuccess

Instagram is obviously all about the visuals. It is a great place to post an honest and behind the scenes look at the life of an author. You can share photos of your work area, your office, a desk scene, a screenshot of a work in progress, your books in the wild (spotting your book in stores), selfies, family pics, photos of your pets (cats of Instagram is popular), photos from signings, conventions and meetings with other authors.

Pinterest is quickly addicting. You can pin all kinds of fun visuals. It is a great tool for authors to create boards for their books. You can create inspiration boards, scenescapes, character inspirations or character styles, background and setting boards, locations, and other visuals. Share the boards with your readers so they get a behind the scenes look into your vision. You can also grab embed codes for individual boards and add them to a guest blog for a tour or to your bonus page on your blog.

Tumblr is another site heavy on visuals. It's like a cross between Pinterest and a Blog. You can share photos and images and your dashboard will give you a feed of everyone's posts that you follow. Tumblr is a great way to connect with fandoms. If you write YA there are many, many, many Tumblr pages devoted entirely to YA. And YA readers are rabid fans and love to create visuals for their favorite books. Tumblr is a great place to share character sketches, dream cast ideas, fan art and book teasers.

Snapchat is an app you can download for Android or iPhone. It's like a text/social media hybrid very popular with the younger crowd, so it is a very good resource if you are a young author or an author of YA books.

Google+ is another social media outlet you should have. It is great for sharing posts and they have hangouts- which means you can create a live event and invite others to join in. If you love to connect live with readers, take advantage of this.

Goodreads is a great site for authors to utilize for advertising and book giveaways. Just don't get too caught up in review drama. Reviews are important, but not important enough to ruin your good standing as an author by freaking out over a bad review. My advice- don't ever comment or respond to bad reviews, it never goes well for an author who does. You can't please everyone, and while bad reviews can feel very personal, they aren't. Accept constructive criticism and use it to your advantage. Just ignore and move on when it comes to bad review trolls who have nothing nice to say about anything.

Other up and coming social media sites to try are **Tsu**, **Booklikes**, and **Booktropolous**. All are relatively new and still growing. Booklikes and Booktropolous are all about books. Booklikes lets you create a blog to post reviews and book information. Booktropolous is like Facebook but strictly for books. Tsu is another Facebook knockoff that many people are enjoying. However, they do not allow blatant promotional posts.

Tips for Email and Social Media Accounts

I work with authors every day- many are first time and indie authors. So I see a lot of mistakes, faux pas, and things that flat out make me cringe.

And no I'm not pointing fingers or trying to shame anyone because I've been there. I've made many of the mistakes, learned from them and moved on. Now I am sharing my wisdom with others.

The number one most important thing to understand when creating your accounts and emails is that in the publishing world we brand the author, not the book. There will be more than one book, more than one series, perhaps even more than one genre. So ultimately you need to focus on author branding, not book branding.

Make sure your web presence reflects this.

Social Media Profiles

Do not make your Twitter name, Facebook profile or any other social media account the title of your book or series. Unless it is the only book or series you ever plan to write. And who starts a writing career with that goal?

You should work on branding yourself as an author- all of your social media accounts should be your name.

In fact, when starting out as a new author (or if you are newly focusing on author branding), everything should be your author name: your website URL, your professional author email, your blog, everything.

Example: I am Roxanne Rhoads across the board- all my social media accounts, my website, my email- it is all Roxanne Rhoads. I can easily be found as Roxanne Rhoads when someone Googles me or searches on Facebook, Pinterest, Twitter, etc.

Once you have started building your author brand you can branch out and create pages, groups, etc. to promote a book or series. Once I built everything as Roxanne Rhoads I added pages and social media dedicated to Bewitching Book Tours.

When promoting your book via social media add in a little extra promotion with hashtagging. Using a hash tag is an easy way to find other posts on the topic you tagged. You can click the hashtag and see if anyone else is talking about your book or series.

Twitter Example: "New release: Hex and the City by @RoxanneRhoads Vehicle City Vampires Book 2 #hexandthecity #vehiclecityvampires"

Notice that I linked to my twitter profile and hash tagged both my book title and series name.

Author Email

A big pet peeve of mine is author emails- I understand you may be working with pen names or perhaps you've had a certain email address forever…but you really need something professional and something easy to remember when someone in the professional book world needs to email you.

Example: if someone were to email me, they could easily remember that I'm roxannerhoads@aol.com or roxannerhoads@bewitchingbooktours.com. It would be harder to find me if I was cutebunny67@yahoo.com.

Sure, that email address might have been cute when you were 18 but now you're trying to be a professional. Please create an email address that reflects your professional author status.

When I am emailing an author I work with, I type in their name and hope autofill or my contact list pulls it up. If they have some weird, out there address it won't show up. Then I have to go searching, which takes time.

If they use their name, bingo it pops up, easy peasy -saves me having to search for it. Professionals love things that are streamlined and make their jobs easier.

So please, grab a professional email address. You can get them free through numerous sources. And don't use your real name address if you are working under your pen name. That is confusing, too. Create an email specifically for your author name.

If you buy a domain name you can even point it to that. I have a domain name (bewitchingbooktours.com) and pay Gmail for their email service to point to my domain-roxannerhoads@bewitchingbooktours.com.

It streamlines everything.

Secrets of Successful Virtual Book Tours

Chapter 3: What To Expect From a Virtual Book Tour

Unrealistic Expectations

Don't sign up for a virtual book tour with unrealistic expectations.

This means- don't expect a tour to make your book a bestseller. Don't expect your book to be blasted across hundreds of sites or become a trending topic.

If you hire a tour company, read the fine print, understand how they operate and what exactly they offer and what they'll be doing to promote your tour and your book. If they send you documents and paperwork- please read it. Chances are the items they send will clear up any confusion and answer 99% of your questions.

Another thing- don't expect someone else to do all the work. Even if you hire a company to schedule the tour you have to provide your book and author materials, provide content for the tour, and you should be promoting yourself daily throughout the tour.

A common misconception authors have, is that they don't have to do anything for the tour- that's what they're hiring a company for. Truth is, you are hiring the company to schedule and organize everything which will save you time, but you'll still have to put some hours in to make sure your tour is successful.

Book Tours and Sales

Many authors think the main goal of a book tour is sales. Of course, that's every author's end goal with any type of advertising.

Usually, a tour does help increase sales but sadly this is not always the case.

Start a tour with networking and increased exposure as your goal and you won't be disappointed. Think of it as establishing name/brand recognition. It's like an online convention- you get to virtually meet readers, bloggers, and other authors which increase your network but doesn't necessarily create sales, at least not right away.

During a tour your books and author name are repeatedly put in front of readers, if you do a giveaway (which I highly recommend) the entries will help increase social media following, and you establish new followers and new connections.

This, in the long run, will translate into sales even if it doesn't seem apparent right away.

A good book tour will never be a waste of time, even if you didn't sell one book.

Why? Because you made connections, you increased exposure, you put yourself out there, you networked with bloggers, reviewers and readers and you made your name known.

You are creating brand recognition. Maybe this book didn't sell a bunch of copies during the tour but your name will be recognized when the next book comes out or when a reader meets you at an event. It will translate to sales in the long run.

Plus you should have content you can use. A good tour company creates a professional media kit with all your book and author information in one place that you can distribute to future promotion locations. Hopefully, you'll also have some great quotes you can pull from reviews to help you promote your book. Remember to always attribute the quote to the reviewer who wrote it and if possible, include a link to the original review.

If you wrote guest blogs or other promotional materials (character profiles, book soundtracks, the story behind the story posts, etc.) you now have content you can reuse on your blog or website as bonus materials. Yes, your guest blogs and other tour materials that you created are yours. You retain copyright to them. Now if a blogger adds their own images, comments or other materials you cannot reuse the blog exactly as it appeared on their site without permission. You retain the rights only to your original creations.

I suggest waiting, at least, a month after your tour ends before reposting any materials to your sites, that way it does not hurt the tour blog's traffic.

Interviews are not the same, not unless you provided both the questions and answers (for instance a character interview you created). If you wish to repost an interview it is in good form to get permission from the blogger who interviewed you. Ask if it is okay to republish the entire interview. Or simply post a link to the interview. And never use a blogger's graphics without permission. I know several bloggers who create custom graphics for book tour stops. They may include book quotes, author quotes from interviews or guest blogs, or review quotes. Those graphics are owned by the blogger. Please ask if you may reprint them on your site or through social media.

Chapter 4: Secrets for a Successful Book Tour

Now that we've gone through the basics of creating an online presence and preparing to tour, you need to know what to do to get the most out of a virtual tour.

Your tour should have a variety of tour stops- many of the blogs or websites you appear on should be genre specific but you also want a mix of basic book blogs that cover anything book related and sites that cover many topics- like an entertainment site that showcases books, music, movies and TV or mommy sites that review products and books. So yes, make sure the tour stops target genre readers and bloggers but don't be afraid to step outside the niche, you never know where you may find a new reader.

Plan your tour as early as possible. Many blog tour companies need one to two months lead time to effectively set up and schedule your book tour. If you are touring during Halloween (for paranormal and horror books) or the winter holidays plan to schedule your tour, at least, two months in advance. Many blogs do special holiday themed posts and their schedules fill fast.

If you are planning on setting up your own tour you may want to start at least three months in advance.

Decide on the length of your tour. Tour companies offer many packages featuring tours of varying lengths- from one day to two months. The most popular tour packages are one day, one week, two weeks and one month tours.

One day tours- often called blitzes or blasts- are best for cover reveals and release day announcements. Longer tours are great for focusing on author branding and putting your book in front of as many readers and possible.

Provide a review copy. Always offer a review copy to tour hosts. No, you don't have to provide print copies, 99% of reviewers now accept e-copies for review.

Not every blogger will decide to review but a good tour should add a minimum of five new reviews. I understand that doesn't sound like a lot but several quality reviews are worth more than many fake or one line reviews. Beware of tour companies that guarantee a certain number of reviews for a tour, many times these end up being canned reviews or fake reviews that don't give your book a good ranking or any good quotes to use for promotions.

When planning the tour, offer host only tour incentives. This increases the number of hosts for your tour. The host incentive is a giveaway only tour hosts can enter. For instance offer a $20 Amazon Gift Card. One tour host will be chosen randomly at the end of the tour. Everyone who hosts a tour stop will be entered. You can add a bonus entry for tour hosts that also review the book- that way they get two entries. Either you or your tour company can create a Rafflecopter form or Google Form to keep track of tour stops and review links.

Plan to offer a tour wide giveaway. Giveaways are not necessary but are highly recommended. This is how you will get the increase of social media followers and newsletter subscribers. Giveaways can be books, eBooks (though I don't suggest giving away more than 5 copies of the book you are touring, you don't want to cut into sales. If you wish to give away a book I suggest something from your backlist instead of the current book on tour.), prize packs, book swag, or Gift Cards. Gift cards and unique prize packs garner the largest number of entries.

Rafflecopter forms or other similar contest form widgets are best for tours. This way a program will keep track of all entries and you (or the tour company) can easily pick winners at the end of the tour. Entry options should include following you on your social media platforms and subscribing to your newsletter as well as sharing the tour stop and giveaway through social media. Many tour companies will create these for you.

At the time of the tour, your book should have a live buy link- this can be a pre-order link or a live, on sale, link.

(This is not necessary for cover reveals). Creating an early buzz for your book can be good, but sometimes it can fizzle out if you do it too early. Create buzz ahead of time through social networking and advertising. Your best bet is to have your book available for purchase during a tour so you get impulse buys from the readers at tour stops.

Coincide Sale Dates or Kindle Free Days with the tour dates. One way to get the most bang for your buck is to coordinate sales and free dates with your tour. Discount your book for the duration of the tour or for just a few days.

Make sure the days your book is free or on sale are heavily promoted during the tour.

Schedule promotion dates at BookBub, BuckBooks, KindleNationDaily, Pixel Of Ink, Author Marketing Club, Awesome Gang, Ereader News Today, Book Lemur, and BookBrag. Most of these sites offer promotion deals for books that are free or highly discounted. These sites offer databases that readers can visit every day for book deals as well as daily emails to their subscribers of current free and sale priced books. Many of the sites do charge fees for this service.

Create Content That Will Draw in Readers

I know many authors are swamped with writing the next book or with a "day job". They need to promote but don't really have enough time to focus on it so they schedule blitzes or promotional tours that offer only basic book details and excerpts for the tour.

This can work for name recognition, repeat exposure and simply for putting your book details out there, but if you want a highly successful tour you have to put in the effort to make it great.

The most important ingredient of a highly successful book tour is content that will draw in the readers.

Engaging content and visuals grab reader attention. This means guest blogs and graphics.

I suggest creating teasers or hiring someone that can create teasers and images for you book.

Teasers are visuals that usually contain a line or two from the book or a review quote, something that will really draw the reader in.

Other creative and engaging content I've seen authors create are maps, character sketches, and custom artwork, even a tarot reading graphic for their tours. These tours had higher traffic ratings than those who provided regular text content.

Create Engaging Guest Blogs, Character Interviews, and Lists

An author guest blog does not have to be a long essay that rambles on about the book or author. Instead, it can be fun, informative and tie in with pop culture, current events, or holidays. This is how to effectively grab a reader's attention, draw them in, connect then introduce them to your book.

For instance, if you write paranormal romance or other vampire fiction (urban fantasy, horror) write a guest post about your Top Ten Favorite Vampire Movies and TV Shows. This will draw in other vampire fans, you will connect with them through shared interests, then they will realize your book is vampire fiction and it might be something they'll like. Bam you just got a sale and hopefully a new fan.

More details about writing guest blogs featured in the next chapter.

Content Tips

While writing your book or series save all of your research materials, outlines, music playlists, character profiles, deleted scenes, inspiration boards, etc.

All of this content can be used to create guest blogs for tours and for bonus material on your website and blog.

My advice- if you know you are going to do a book tour, use the materials on tour first. Provide something new at every stop. Give readers a reason to follow your tour. Give them exclusive, never before seen content.

After the tour, you can repurpose the content on your website or blog and in your newsletter.

A Note on Images

Make sure that you have the proper rights to any images you use for the tour- this means that you either own the rights to the image or have permission to use it.

The safest way to do this is to provide images that are yours- which means you are either the photographer or artist that created the image.

You can also purchase rights to use images from numerous sites around the web. If you want unique custom art you can often find great images on Deviant Art and contact the artist to get permission to use their work. Sometimes they will charge a fee for this.

There are many stock photo sites that you can purchase stock images from.

You can also find free to use, copyright free and creative commons images at Pixabay, Unsplash, and PublicDomainPictures.net.

Always keep track of where you got an image from. Keep purchase receipts from stock sites and always get artist or photographer permissions in writing if the images came from somewhere other than a stock site. Some authors find custom artwork on DeviantArt and purchase rights from the artists to use their designs or photographs.

Keep all receipts and permissions in a file in case anyone ever questions if you have the rights to use an image.

Using Celebrity Images

Authors often want to use celebrity images to cast their characters either just as an example of how the author visualizes the character or who she would cast if the book were to become a movie or TV show.

Copyrights on celebrity images can be tricky- some images are distributed for the media to use. So if you were to get an image from a media wire source, use the image as is, and attribute the image correctly to the source (the photographer or other copyright owner). That should cover you legally.

But if you were to make graphics with these images or change them in any way (for example using them on teasers) then you are stepping over the line.

Same goes for purchasing celebrity images on stock sites. Yes, you can use the image on your blog or in content but you can't put the image on a resale item or something used for selling items.

And never, ever use a celebrity image on your book cover unless you or your publisher hired the celebrity to appear on the cover.

When in doubt contact an attorney that specializes in copyrights. Many have free Q&A's online.

Content Creation Timeframe

Prepare your materials in advance or as soon as you receive your tour schedule.

Don't wait until the last minute to send your content to your tour company or to the blogs you scheduled stops with. Many bloggers schedule their tour stops at least a week in advance. Please plan to provide your final tour stop content no later than 7 days before the scheduled stop.

What To Provide to Tour Hosts

Every tour host should receive a media kit, excerpt, book tour banner, and giveaway details for your tour. If you hired a tour company they should create and put all these details together for you and send them to hosts.

Always label documents precisely. For example- your media kit should be labeled as "Media Kit Your Book Title by Your Author Name".

Tour content should be labeled with the name of the blog and your book title or author name. "Diane's Book Blog Guest Blog from Author Name December 14".

Be as specific as possible, this will help tremendously when it comes to keeping things organized whether for yourself or the blog tour company, not to mention it'll make things so much easier for the blog tour hosts.

If a tour stop is scheduled to post unique content provide that host with their additional requested materials (guest blog, interview, vlog, etc.). For tour posts that include images- provide the image in the document as well as an attached jpeg. Some people can pull images from documents while others can't. It all depends on program compatibility and operating systems.

If you hire a tour company to set up your tour make sure they offer the creation of a professional media kit and tour banners as part of your package. This saves you time on creating content for each of the hosts.

Banners and tour buttons should feature your book cover, tour dates and the logo for the book company that organized the tour. If you handle your own tour make sure you have a graphic that features your book cover and the tour dates.

Media kits should contain your book and author details in one convenient place- book title, author name, publisher name, genre, release date, number of words and/or pages in the book, the book's description, book purchase links and an author bio, image and author web and social media links. Media kits for tours also usually contain a short excerpt and, if available, review quotes.

What to Do During the Tour

During the tour promote your stops daily. If you hired a tour company they should be promoting the tour stops heavily but you also want to promote yourself. Share the tour stops with your social media network. Post a schedule on the events page of your blog or website and send out a newsletter about your tour. Create an event page on Facebook and share links and details every day of the tour.

Encourage everyone to participate in stops and giveaways. If you created unique content, readers will have something new to discover every day of your tour.

Thank your tour hosts. You would be surprised how much a simple thank you can mean to a blogger who took the time to post your book tour materials. Either leave a comment on the tour stop or send them a thank you via email. This will help bloggers remember you and they'll be more likely to help you promote during future tours and new book releases.

Chapter 5: An Author's Guide to Writing Great Guest Blogs

What is a Guest Blog?

Think of a guest blog as a personal essay, article, or blog post about anything related to you and/or your book.

The key to a good guest blog is to make it interesting and entertaining without being overly promotional. You want it to tie into your book or series without being a post that says nothing more than "buy my book".

Entertain readers, grab their attention-connect with them.

Some authors blog about their road to being an author, or the creation of the book, the inspiration behind it.

Many authors tie in popular topics to their books, for instance the popularity of vampires, recent crime, upcoming holidays, current events, etc.

You could also focus on a specific character or the location setting. Some people use pictures and images from places that are actually images from the town the book is set in or they find great images to represent them.

One way to think of the guest blog is as bonus material for the book.

Think of the bonus material you would find on a movie DVD- deleted scenes, bloopers (fun stuff), soundtrack, interviews with characters, book trailer, etc.

You can also use other materials in place of the traditional essay style guest blog: lists, recipes, character profiles, character interviews. Anything fun that ties into your book.

The average length of a good guest blog is between 300-500 words. Anything shorter and it seems rushed, longer and you may lose attention unless you have it broken up with bold headers, sections or numbered lists. 1000-2000 words are good if you have a great topic you wish to discuss in depth and you can make it web friendly with bold headings, bullet points, and short paragraphs.

Writing the Guest Blog

No matter what style of guest blog you choose to write, whether a traditional essay post, an article, a character interview, or a list- **it should always have a beginning, middle and end.**

Always provide an intro, something that introduces you, your book, or your guest blog topic.

Here's an example of an intro for a top ten list style post:

Hello, my name is Author Supernatural and I write vampire romance novels. Today I'd like to discuss some of my favorite vampires in television and movies.

The middle section would be your list of favorite vampires- it would be good to discuss them a little and tell readers why they are your favorite.

After your list, you should provide a closer, an end to your guest blog.

A good way to close it is with a question that will engage readers and encourage them to comment on the post and interact with you.

A closer question for this vampire top ten list could be: "Who are your favorite vampires from TV or movies?"

Examples of Popular Guest Blog Topics

Fun, Bonus Material Topics:

Music Playlist (book soundtrack)

Character Profiles (including photos or artwork is great for visual effect)

Character Interviews

Deleted Scenes

Alternate Endings

The Story Behind the Story

The Book Setting (do you have fun details or interesting visuals that can help readers connect to the setting of the book, is the setting in a real location you can include maps and photos of?)

5 Facts about My Book That Might Surprise You

An Excerpt with a Bit of Backstory or an Intro to the Scene

Author Centric Topics:

When I'm Not Writing (do you have any fun interests, hobbies, or things you do when you're not writing)

Authors That Have Inspired Me

My Favorite Books of all Time

My Inspiration: The Things in Life That Inspire Me

A Day in the Life of…(you could also do this for a character)

Creating a Memorable Character

Create (or Find a Recipe for) a Cocktail Based on One of Your Characters.

Create a Pinterest -Style Board- Use Images that are Meaningful to One of Your Characters or the Story in General.

Dream Movie Cast if the Novel Became a Film

Tips for Novice Writers

Things I Love to Hear My Readers Say

The Ultimate Leading Man

Top 10 Things You Need to Write

Fun Topics That Are Genre Related:

Top 10 Fictional Book Characters of All Time

Top 10 Vampires in Books

Top 10 Vampires in the Movies

Sexiest Vampires of all Time

Sexiest Shifters of All Time

Top 10 Favorite Books

Top Ten Favorites (Paranormal, Vampire, insert your topic) Movies (or Books)

Hottest Vamps on TV

The Best Witches on Television and in the Movies

The Fictional Characters I Would Invite to a Party

Vampires with Style: The Best Dressed Vamps of All Time

Animal Appeal: Why We Love Shifters

If I was A Shifter What Animal Would I Be?

The Alpha Male: Why We Love Him

Secrets of Successful Virtual Book Tours

Favorite Alpha Males

Alpha Females- Rise of Strong Female Characters

If I Could Have One Magic Power It Would Be…

Dragons – Good or Bad?

What Makes Your Dragons Different?

I Love Dragons Because…

History of Dragons

Top 10 Dragons in Literature

Top 10 Dragons in Television and Movies

Top 10 Fairytales

Top Ten YA Books

Best Book to Movie Crossovers

Heroes Versus Villains- The Best Match Ups

The Anti-Hero

Steampunk Tea- Characters to Invite to a Tea Party

Steampunk Gadgets- My Favorite Fictional Technology

Alternate History- Creating a Steampunk World

Holiday Ties Ins:

Vampire Valentine Gift Guide

Book Characters I Would Invite to a Halloween Party

Halloween Party Costumes

Christmas Gifts for Vampires

Christmas Gifts for Vampire Lovers

Witchy Holiday Gifts

Ten Ways Witches Celebrate Halloween

Werewolf Holiday Shopping Guide

A Gift Guide for Fairies

Under the Sea Gift Ideas for Mermaids and Water Creatures

Why Leprechauns Hate/Love St. Patrick's Day

Horror Tales for Halloween

Character Focused Guest Blogs:

An Introduction to (a character from your book)

A Day in the Life of My Character

5 Things I Could Give My Character for (His/Her) Birthday

The Author Vlog

If you have a webcam and are tech friendly (and not camera shy) I suggest trying a vlog.

It's not as scary as it sounds. If you have a webcam and high-speed internet it's fairly easy. Record the video and upload to YouTube.

This is a fun way to interact with readers. You can record a short piece about your book, perhaps include a short reading from the book and upload to YouTube where tour hosts can grab embed codes and add it to their site for a guest spot along the tour.

Another type of vlog feature is where readers send in questions about you or your book beforehand and you can answer the questions in your recording.

Chapter 6: Tips for Planning Your Own Virtual Book Tour

If you decide to plan your own virtual book tour you'll still need to heed all the previous advice but in addition to that, you'll need to find the bloggers and reviewers to host your tour.

Luckily instead of just googling book blogs or genre book blogs, there are a few databases you can access for free that will help you find book bloggers that might host your tour. The Book Blogger Directory, Book Blogger List, YA Book Blog Directory, and The Indie View all have lists of book bloggers you can contact.

Here are direct URLs to the sites:

https://bookbloggerdirectory.wordpress.com/

http://bookbloggerlist.com/

http://yabookblogdirectory.blogspot.com/p/ya-book-blogger-list.html

http://www.theindieview.com/indie-reviewers/

Before Contacting Bloggers

Here's a little review from the previous chapters.

Before you start setting up your tour make sure your website and social media accounts are created and up to date. Be sure all your links work on your website and blog. Double check that all your info is correct on all sites.

Create a media kit and basic tour content ahead of time- this includes tour banners, book teasers, excerpts, book trailer, Pinterest boards (grab the embed code for boards), and basic guest blogs.

Have review copies ready to send, these can be ARCs but label them as such so reviewers don't think they are final copies. This way they don't judge possible spelling errors or grammar issues that should be cleared up after the final edits. Have multiple formats available. The most common are pdf, epub, and Mobi formats. Other options include sending a NetGalley widget (if you use the NetGalley service) or a Smashwords coupon code so they can download the format of their choice for free directly from Smashwords.

Keep all of your tour materials organized in a file folder on your computer. That way everything is in one place and easy to find.

Advice for Contacting Bloggers and Reviewers

First of all, create one professional email template to send to everyone you will approach about participating in your tour. The email should be professional and polite. Introduce yourself and your book. This is where having a short tagline or two line pitch for the book comes in handy. Something quick that will grab their attention.

Let them know you are planning a virtual book tour (include the dates) and you would love it if they could host a stop. Include the types of stops that are available (guest blogs, interviews, top ten lists, book trailer, etc.) and the formats of the review copies available (pdf, epub, Mobi, Smashwords coupon, Kindle gift copy, etc.).

After this include a longer description of the book, buy links to the book at Amazon, BN, Smashwords, etc. (if they are available), your author bio and links to your author website. If you have a couple eye catching review quotes for the book, include them.

Close with a polite, thank you I look forward to hearing from you (or something similar).

~Author name
Author email address

Never send a bunch of attachments or a review copy of the book in the first email. If they agree to review or to be a tour host, then you can send attachments and your book. Always send a confirmation email which includes the tour stop and date along with tour materials.

The second thing you need to do is create a database of the blogs you will contact. The database should include blog names, URLs, and contact emails.

You can either create a spreadsheet or list, whichever you are more comfortable with. You can check off each blog after you send them an email. You may want to include the date you sent the email so you can follow up if you don't receive a response after a week or so. If they do respond and agree to participate in the tour add the details of your tour stop on your list as well as adding them to your schedule.

This leads us to the third thing you need to create, your tour schedule. Your schedule needs to include the date of the tour stop, type of stop, name of the blog along with its URL, and the blogger's email address. Make a note of what materials you need to send to them (guest blog, interview, teasers, etc.). Create a note or add a check mark when you send completed materials to them.

Once your tour is scheduled, send all necessary materials to your blogs hosts.

Post your tour schedule on your website, blog, and social media accounts.

During the tour check in every morning to make sure your tour stop is posted.

Share the direct URL links of the tour stops throughout social media. Check in a couple times a day to see if anyone has posted comments or questions for you.

If a tour host did not post as agreed send them a gentle reminder email along with the tour materials. Hopefully, they post, most do. Missed tour stops often result from a simple oversight, scheduling error, or technical glitch. Understand that sometimes bloggers simply disappear into cyberspace never to be heard from again. Don't take it personally if they do.

Chapter 7: Are Real World Events Things of the Past?

Real world events are not a thing of the past.

By all means go out to local bookstores, libraries, seasonal and holiday events and set up signings, schedule fun events that will bring people in- work with other authors to create group events that will draw a crowd.

For instance, if you write paranormal books- get out there at Halloween events and sell your stuff. Set up tables for sales and signings at Halloween readings and parties at local libraries, (schools too if your book is kid oriented), hayrides, even haunted houses.

Work with your community to promote your book. You might be surprised at how many local businesses and event planners will be thrilled to have something unique and special (like an author) be a guest at their holiday event. I have found that local wineries, cafes, and specialty gift boutiques are very open to cultural events. They love to have local authors and artists hold events at their venues.

And be sure to bring business cards, bookmarks or even book trading cards, to all your live book promotions. Pass them out at local libraries and bookstores too.

The key is- get out there and promote your book- whether virtually, in real life, or both. You are not going to get anywhere as an author being a hermit and hiding in your house tapping away at the keys of your computer.

Publication is only the beginning of the process…promotion is the road to success.

About the Author

Story strumpet, tome loving tart, eccentric night owl...these words describe book publicist and erotic romance author Roxanne Rhoads.

When not fulfilling one the many roles being a wife and mother of three require, Roxanne's world revolves around words...reading them, writing them, editing them, and talking about them. In addition to writing her own stories she loves to read, promote and review what others write.

Roxanne is the owner of Bewitching Book Tours and operates Fang-tastic Books, a book blog dedicated to paranormal and urban fantasy books.

When not reading, writing, or promoting Roxanne loves to hang out with her family, craft, garden and search for unique vintage finds.

Visit her online

Author Website http://www.roxannerhoads.com
Book Blog www.fang-tasticbooks.blogspot.com
Bewitching Book Tours www.bewitchingbooktours.com

Afterword: Consider Bewitching Book Tours

Bewitching Book Tours has been in business since 2010 making us one of the oldest virtual book tour companies around. We know book promotion.

Our authors are our number one priority. This is not a hobby or a side job in addition to the day job. This is our day job, which means we put our authors first.

Bewitching Book Tours offers multiple tour packages and services for authors- we have one day packages for cover reveals, release day blitzes, and one day tours. We also offer one week, two week and one-month tours.

Bewitching offers Kindle Free Book Blitz tours to promote your Kindle free book for up to five days. Other services we offer are Twitter parties, Facebook parties, Press Release Writing, and radio interviews.

Custom packages are available for authors, publicists, and publishers.

Bewitching Book Tours has special features including a monthly magazine, a BlogTalk Radio Show and custom

Bewitching Book swag creations such as bookmarks, keychains, earrings and purse charms.

One of the stand-out features of Bewitching Book Tours is that your book starts receiving promotion as soon as you sign up with Bewitching. A media kit is created, tour banners are made, and a page goes up on the Bewitching Blog announcing your upcoming tour.

An invitation is sent out to all the Bewitching Tour Hosts that subscribe to our host only newsletter and your upcoming tour is shared throughout our vast network of social media which includes multiple Facebook pages and accounts, Tsu, Twitter, Google +, Pinterest, Tumblr, and other book social sites.

Immediately your book has been put in front of thousands of book lovers. And we don't stop there. We continue to work on your tour scheduling tour stops, reviews and more depending on the tour package chosen.

Once your tour is set up we will send you the tour schedule, materials and instructions so there is no confusion on what is expected of you as an author. You return all requested materials to Bewitching and we handle the rest.

Once your tour has started we promote every single tour stop every day on multiple social media platforms several times throughout the day. Combine this exposure with the daily tour hosts and then add the author's own social media promotion- and the tour can reach thousands of readers every day.

An author will have quality content that can be used after the tour including a professional media kit with all the book and author information in one place that can be distributed to future promotion locations. You'll also have great quotes you can pull from reviews to help you promote your book.

Even after the tour, Bewitching continues working for you. Your name and web link will be listed on our blog as a client and your tour pages will be archived, not removed. So they will always be available for readers to access.

Made in the USA
Middletown, DE
04 January 2018